# THE
# SEATTLE
# JOKE BOOK
# III

by
**Elliot Maxx**

Thanks to
Darryl and Linda Igelmund, Michelle Beaudry,
Michael Brasky, Ron Reid, Laura Crocker, Tim
Gallagher, Betty Holman, Larry Pendergast and,
of course, to all my comedian buddies who make
this kind of project a lot of fun.

Special thanks to
My wife and kids for putting up with me
while I put this together.

And an extra special thanks to
Gene Openshaw
A good friend and a very funny man.

The Seattle Joke Book

ISBN # 0-935735-06-2

This book is dedicated to
# The Spotted Owl
who gave his home so these words
could be published.

# Contents

# The
# Seattle
# Joke
# Book
# III

"The nicest winter I ever spent
was a summer on Puget Sound."
**Mark Twain**

**SEATTLE GOTHIC**

# Seattle

What's the definition of a Seattle optimist?
    A guy with a sunvisor on his rainhat.

Did you hear about the new Gore-Tex tanktop?
    It's called "Sleeveless In Seattle."

"I can't believe it," said the tourist. "I've been here an entire week and it's done nothing but rain. When do you have summer here?"
    "Well, that's hard to say," replied the local. "Last year, it was on a Wednesday."

What does Daylight Savings Time mean in Seattle?
An extra hour of rain.

\*

At a Klan Meeting, how can you tell which guy is from Seattle?
He's wearing rubber sheets.

\*

The morning after a Seattle Symphony fundraising party, one of the musicians was discussing the party with his wife.

"I got so drunk last night," he said, "I forgot to thank the host."

"Well," said his wife, "maybe you should give them a call."

"I would," said the musician, "but I don't even remember where I was."

"What do you remember?" asked his wife.

"Well, it was some really fancy place in the Highlands. In fact, they even had a solid gold toilet."

After coffee, the musician and his wife drove up to the main gate in the Highlands and asked the guard for help. When they recounted the story about the gold toilet, he picked up the phone and dialed.

"Hello, Mr. Nelson," he said into the receiver, "This is John down at the gate. I think we found the guy who crapped in your tuba."

## ANOTHER ROADSIDE ATTRACTION

**NO PARKING ANY TIME**

### CAUTION
### You Are Now Entering Downtown

\*

What is the most popular sight to see in Seattle?
> An empty parking place.

\*

What do you call a gravel parking lot in downtown Seattle?
> A diamond in the rough.

\*

What do you get when you cross Joe Diamond and "Almost Live!"
> A barrel of laughs.

**Another unsuspecting tourist is caught in the crossfire at The Pike Place Fish Market.**

A poor, young tourist named Tarkett
Drove his car to the Pike Place Market
Instead of seeing the sights
He spent all day and all night
Just finding a place to park it

Why do they throw the fish at the Pike Place Market?
>So tourists can bring them home and say, "Look what I caught!"

\*

What do you call the birds that hang around the Starbucks?
>The Swallows of Capuccino.

\*

What's the difference between Starbucks and regular coffee?
>About two bucks a cup.

\*

How can you tell you've had too much to drink at The Space Needle Restaurant?
>When the room *stops* spinning.

\*

What's ruder than having a waiter at the Space Needle give you the razzberry?
>Having the chef at Benihana's give you the finger.

\*

Have you tried the new Kingdome Peanut Butter?
>It doesn't stick to the roof of your mouth.

An out of work bouncer went into the Fenix Underground to apply for a job.

"They get pretty rowdy around here," said the bartender. "Do you think you can handle yourself?"

"Just watch," said the bouncer. Then he walked over to an especially loudmouth drunk at the back of the club, lifted him off his feet and threw him sprawling into the street. Returning to the bar, he asked, "How's that?"

"Great!" said the bartender, "but you'll have to talk to the boss about hiring. I just work here."

"Fine," said the bouncer. "Where is he?"

"Just coming back in the front door."

\*

The Empty Space Theatre opened their season with a terrible production. It was a very tense time for everyone involved. On opening night, the cast was fighting and arguing backstage. When the director walked in and saw them, he said, "You people are acting very badly."

"Oh yeah?" said one of the cast members. "Well, you're not much of a director, either."

\*

What's the difference between Wagner's "Ring" and a root canal?

A root canal is not an annual event.

A young guy trying to impress his date suggested taking in the Seattle Art Museum.

"Fabulous," said the young lady.  "I hear they have a new exhibit on Impressionism."

"Great," said the guy.  "I love Impressionism."

"Really?  Tell me -- who is your favorite impressionist?"

"I dunno," said the guy.  "Rich Little, I guess."

*"The orchestra appreciates your enthusiasm, however, we feel "The Wave" may be an inappropriate response to Brahams' Symphony No.4 in E minor."*

What's white and splatters on your umbrella?
    Bumberpoop.

*

A guy sits down next to a girl at a downtown bus stop.
    "Hi," he says. "My name's Bill. What's yours?"
    "Sandy," says the girl.
    "What do you do for a living?" he asks.
    "I'm an actress," says Sandy, smiling.
    "Oh, really?" says Bill. "Which restaurant?"

*

A grunge rocker was charged with assault and battery at a Pearl Jam Concert.
    After the opening remarks, the judge looked at the prosecutor and said, "Are you trying to tell me this guy assaulted a woman in the middle of the Gas Works Park, in front of 3000 people?
    "Yes, your honor." said the prosecutor.
    "Why didn't anyone try to stop him?" asked the judge.
    "Well, sir," replied the prosecutor, "everyone thought they were dancing."

*

What's the most popular band on Snoqualmie Pass?
    Alice in Snow Chains.

What's the quickest way to drive through Seattle?
　　The Espresso Lanes.

＊

A tourist from Eastern Washington walks up to an espresso stand.
　　"I'd like a cup of coffee, please."
　　"Espresso or latte'?"
　　"Latte'."
　　"Columbian or European Roast?"
　　"Columbian."
　　"Single or double?"
　　"Single."
　　"Regular or decaf?"
　　"Regular."
　　"With or without?"
　　"With."
　　"Cream or half-n-half?"
　　"I'll have tea."

＊

A lady stopped at a little coffeeshop in Belltown. As she sat down, an elderly Italian gentleman behind the counter grabbed the coffee pot and began to pour.
　　"You want summa coffee?" he asked.
　　"Actually," she said, "I'd prefer a latte'."
　　"Sure, lady," he said, setting down the pot, "you canna have as mucha you like."

## Northwest Evolution Chart

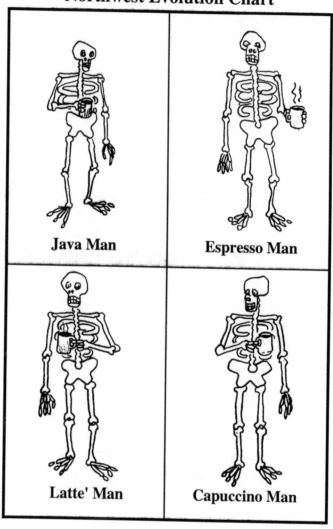

Java Man      Espresso Man

Latte' Man      Capuccino Man

One particularly dreary Seattle afternoon, a depressed young woman decided to end her life by throwing herself into Elliott Bay.

When she went down to the Waterfront, a young sailor noticed her crying and took pity on her.

"Look," he said. "I'm going on a cruise to the South Pacific in the morning, and if you like, you can stow away on my ship. You can start a new life, there. I'll take good care of you and bring you food everyday."

Moving closer, he slipped his arm around her shoulder and added, "I'll keep you happy and you keep me happy."

The girl decided to go along with the idea. What did she have to lose?

That night, the sailor brought her aboard and hid her in a lifeboat. Every night after that, he brought her food and they made mad passionate love until dawn.

A few weeks later, she was discovered by the captain.

"What are you doing in this lifeboat?" he asked.

"I had an arrangement with one of your crew," she explained. "He said he was taking me to the South Pacific, and every night he came in and screwed me."

"He sure did, lady." said the captain. "This is the Winslow Ferry."

## ANOTHER ROADSIDE ATTRACTION

| Warning sign on most major highways | Warning sign on Interstate 5 |

**\***

Did you hear about Seattle's newest Freeway Park? It's called "rush hour."

**\***

What's the difference between a Northwest Car Dealer and a theif?

A thief rarely offers 3.9% financing.

**\***

What's the difference between 911 and Domino's Pizza?

When you dial Domino's, they will usually respond in 30 minutes for less.

How can you tell that your car needs a tune-up?

> When you're downtown and you actually get pulled over by one of those cops on bikes.

∗

What's more embarrassing than getting pulled over by a cop on a bike?

> Getting arrested and having to ride to the station on the handlebars?

∗

What's even more embarrassing than that?

> Pulling over and discovering it was just a Mormon Missionary.

*"Yes, I'm sure a lot of people do pee in Greenlake, sir, but not from the diving board."*

What does VW stand for in Seattle?
 Virtual Wallingford.

*

What do they call grocery store clerks in the International District?
 Chinese Checkers.

*

What happens when you cross a grunge rocker with a Uwajimaya employee?
 Every December 7th, he attacks Pearl Jam.

*

Why did the original settlers name one of Seattle's neighborhoods Queen Anne?
 Because King Anne sounded stupid.

*"I'm sorry, ma'am, but I don't believe that Stan Boreson is a candidate."*

# Ballard

Two old Norwegian fishermen were talking. The first one said, "I think my wife is dead."

"Are you sure?" asked the second one.

"It's hard to say," replied the first one. "The sex is the same, but the dishes are starting to pile up."

Did you hear Hughes Aircraft is building an airplane in Ballard?

It's called "The Snoose Goose."

Where do Ballard alcoholics go for treatment?

The Betty Fjord Clinic.

An old guy from Ballard was taking his first airplane flight. He seemed quite nervous as he fidgeted with his seatbelt, so the stewardess asked him if she could help.

"Well, I heard the altitude can be pretty rough on your ears," said the old-timer.

"That's true," the stewardess said, handing him a stick of gum, "but I'm sure this'll help."

After the flight, she saw the old man walking through the terminal.

"How was your flight?" she asked.

"Great," said the old man, "but I do have a question?"

"What's that?"

"How do I get the gum out of my ears?"

✳

What's the toughest part of being a Ballard yuppie?
Deciding what wine goes with fishsticks.

✳

How do you get 20 Ballard housewives in a phone booth?
Put a Garage Sale sign on the door.

✳

What is Ballard's favorite drink?
A Martini with a prune.

What's fifty feet long and smells like urine?
Line dancing at the Ballard Senior Center.

✻

What do you call a Biker in Ballard?
Rebel Without A Clue.

✻

An old lady sits down on a bench next to an old man in Bergen Square.

"Guess how old I am," says the old man.

"I don't want to," she replies.

"Please?"

"Well, if you really want me to, you have to take off all your clothes."

The old guy is surprised at her request, but after a moment he takes off his clothes.

"Good," she says. "Now jump up and down and make a noise like a chicken."

He does this, too.

"Good. Now flap your arms. Pretend you're flying. Excellent. You can stop now," she says. "Watching you, I would guess that you're about a month away from your eighty-fifth birthday."

"That's amazing," says the old guy. "You're exactly right! How on earth did you ...?"

"It wasn't that hard," she shrugs. "You told me yesterday."

*"On second thought, that was the down button."*

Did you hear about the new "Ballard Vacation?"
You stay at home and let your mind wander.

*

What do they serve at a Norwegian Deli?
Ballard Lox.

*

Why did the old Swede put condoms on his ears?
He didn't want to get hearing aids.

This kid was working at a store in downtown Ballard. After he had waited on his first customer, the manager decided to give him a few sales pointers.

"You did pretty well," said the manager, "But you need to learn a few things. Watch."

The next customer came to the checkout stand with a bag of grass seed.

"Well, sir," said the manager. "Did you happen to notice we're having a sale on lawn mowers?"

"What would I need a lawn mower for?" asked the customer.

"Well," replied the manager, "from the looks of things, you're going to have quite a yard soon. So you're probably going to need a new mower."

After the customer left with his new mower, the manager turned to the kid.

"See," he said, "there's nothing to it. Now you try that on the next one."

"Okay," said the kid eagerly.

The next customer came to the register with several items, including a box of tampons for his wife. The kid looked at him and said, "Did you notice that we're having a sale on lawn mowers?"

"What would I need a lawn mower for?" asked the bewildered customer.

"Well," said the kid. "From the looks of things, your weekend's shot. So you might as well get some yard work done."

An old Swede was leaving the Tulalip Casino with several bags full of quarters.

"Yumpin' Yiminey," he exclaimed. "I yust can't believe it. I must have hit fifty yackpots in a row!"

Hearing this, one of the casino employees approached him and asked if he needed a ride back to Ballard.

"How did you know I was from Ballard?" asked the Old Swede. "Because of my accent?"

"No, because you've been playing the change machine."

\*

Did you hear about the new Ballard car pool?
    They meet at work.

\*

How can you tell which Seafair Pirate is from Ballard?
    He's the one with a patch over both eyes.

\*

Did you hear about the Ballard lesbian?
    She likes guys.

\*

Why did the Norwegian bring golf balls to an Easter Egg Hunt?
    Decoys.

A criminal from Ballard got arrested for robbing the Crown Hill Bank.

When he was picked out of the lineup, he said to his lawyer, "I don't know how they recognized me. I wore a nylon stocking and everything."

"Well," said the lawyer, "I'm no expert, but next time you might try wearing the nylons on your head."

Why did they close down the Ballard chapter of Alzheimer's Anonymous?

No one could remember where they held the meetings.

How many Ballardites does it take to screw in a lightbulb?

Three. One to screw it in and the others to reminisce about how good the old bulb was.

# Fremont

What's the shortest distance between Seattle and Woodstock?

    The Fremont Bridge.

Did you hear about the new department store opening in Fremont?

    The Bong Marche'.

What's the difference between a sasquatch and a hippie chick from Fremont?

    No matter how loaded you get a sasquatch, he won't dance in front of the stage at a Greatful Dead concert.

What's the difference between a Fremont wedding and a Fremont funeral?

> There's one less Deadhead at the funeral.

\*

How can you spot a seagull from Fremont?

> It's the one with hair under its wings.

\*

What's the difference between the Fremont Sunday Market and a farm auction?

> At most farm auctions, the cows don't wear paisley dresses?

\*

A guy from Fremont was searching for the meaning of life. Hoping to find the answer, he sold all his worldly possessions and hitchhiked to Yelm to contact the long-dead spirit of Ramtha.

When he got there, he was brought to a room filled with candles. Sitting in the center of the room was a woman in a deep trance moaning softly..

"What is the meaning of life?" he asked.

"Life," said the eery voice, "is a river."

He waited in silence, but the spirit said nothing more. Finally he asked, "What do you mean, 'Life is a river?'"

"All right," said the voice, "life is *not* a river."

A hippie chick was standing at a bus stop in Fremont with her breast hanging out of her blouse.

A cop pulled up in his patrol car and said, "Hey, lady! I don't know what you think you're doing, but that kind of thing is really out of line -- even for Fremont!"

"Oh my god!" she exclaimed, looking down at her open blouse. "I left the baby on the bus!"

\*

In Fremont, what's the difference between a Harley and a Hoover?

The position of the dirt bag.

\*

A shriveled, elderly hippie was sitting contentedly on a bench at the Fremont Sunday Market when a young man walked by and said, "You look like you don't have a care in the world."

"I don't," replied the frail, old man.

"Really? What is the secret of your happiness?"

"Well," said the old man, rubbing his whiskers, "I have spent my life following the Greatful Dead wherever they go, drinking, partying, taking drugs and sleeping in my van."

"That's incredible!" exclaimed the young man. "And just how old are you?"

"Twenty-three."

Where do Volkswagen Buses drive on the Freeway?
In the Karma Pool Lane.

\*

## ANOTHER ROADSIDE ATTRACTION

### Seattle Bumpersticker

> # Honk if you love Jesus

### Fremont Bumpersticker

> # Honk if you *are* Jesus

\*

What do you call a Fremont "Rennaisance Man?"
A guy who can smoke pot, read your aura,
and play air guitar at the same time.

\*

How do you handle a labor dispute in Fremont?
Transcendental Mediation.

Did you hear about Fremont's new remedial Palm Reading Course?
>It's called "Hooked on Fingers."

*

Why are the Mariners thinking of building their new natural turf stadium in Fremont?
>Most of the people there have been growing grass indoors for years.

*" ... light-bodied, delicate flavor whose distinctive bouquet makes it a delightful accompaniment to any meal, but especially suited for seafood, chicken or pasta."*

# Pioneer Square

What do you call a wino racing across Pioneer Square?
  Rapid Transient.

*

What do you call a sauna in a homeless shelter?
  A tramp steamer.

*

What do you call a homeshow in Pioneer Square?
  The Street Of Broken Dreams.

Tony Ventrella is walking across Pioneer Square on his way to a motivational seminar one afternoon when a panhandler approaches him for a quarter.

"Sir," asks Tony, "how can you waste your life out here begging for quarters? You are a human being with limitless potential! Where's your dignity? Your pride? Don't you know you are worth so much more than this?"

"Yes, I do," agrees the panhandler, "but a quarter is about all these cheap bastards are willing to part with."

\*

What do you get when you cross a wino with a rhyming dictionary?

A bum rap.

\*

What do you call a soup kitchen with no front door?

Mission Impassible.

\*

A wino shows up at the Lighthouse Mission, cold, sick and hungry. When the social worker sees him, she exclaims, "Oh my God! You look terrible! How did you get in this state?"

"I dunno," said the wino, shaking his head. "I just sobered up and here I was."

A bum goes up to a foreign tourist for a handout.
"Buddy," he says, "could you spare a quarter?"
"What's a quarter?" asks the foreigner.
"You're right," says the bum. "Make it a buck."

\*

What do you call a wino who only comes out at night?

A trampire.

\*

What do judges and winos have in common?

They both spend most of their careers on the bench.

Who was Pioneer Square's first pioneer?
Wyatt Urp.

*

An old wino shows up at Detox one night. The caseworker, having seen him many times before, says, "Ed, this is the fifteenth time we have dried you out. After all our counseling and support, you just keep drinking. How do you explain that?"

"I dunno," shrugs the old wino, "tenacity?"

*

Why do pigeons have wings?
To beat the bums to the cigaret butts.

*

A drunk is staggering along First Avenue with one foot in the gutter and the other on the curb. A cop stops him and says, "I think you're a little too drunk today. Do you know you got one foot in the gutter and one on the sidewalk?"

"Oh, thank God," says the drunk, looking at his feet. "I thought I was going lame."

*

What do you call three winos sleeping in a garbage dumpster?
Menage a' tramp.

An executive from KCTS TV is walking through Pioneer Square when a panhandler approaches him for a handout.

"Excuse me, pal," he says, "could you spare a couple bucks?"

The exec glares at him, "You should be ashamed of yourself -- begging for money like this?"

"I know," replies the panhandler, "but I couldn't get the rights to 'It's a Wonderful Life.'"

# Capitol Hill

What is Capitol Hill's idea of a mixed marriage?
Male and Female.

*

What's black and marches down Broadway?
Martin Luther Queen.

*

A guy sits next to a girl in a Capitol Hill bar.

"Hi," he says. "My name's Bill."

"Look, Bill," says the girl. "I might as well tell you right up front -- I'm a Lesbian."

"Oh really?" says Bill. "What part of Lesbanon are you from?"

What do they call sleeping bags on Capitol Hill?
     Fruit Roll-Ups.

*

How can you tell the Capitol Hill Avon Lady has a crush on you?
     She has an erection.

*

What do you get when you cross a mafia hitman with a Capitol Hill waiter?
     The Quiche of Death.

*

A guy joins a Capitol Hill singles club.

"You're going to like it here," says the manager. "On Monday night, we get together for cocktails."

"I'm sorry," says the guy . "I don't drink."

"Well, that's okay." continues the manager. "On Tuesday, we all get together for casino night."

"I don't gamble, either."

"Well, don't worry. On Wednesday, we bring in some strippers and have a real good time."

"I'm not into that, either."

"You're not gay, are you?"

"No, I'm not gay."

"Oh," says the manager, looking at his schedule, "I guess you're not going to like Thursday, either."

The Captain of The Capitol Hill Fire Station walks in on two firemen making love.

"Hey," he says, "aren't you guys are supposed to be practicing artificial respiration?"

The first fireman looks up and says, "How do you think this got started?"

*

At a chic Capitol Hill restaurant, a customer finds a handwritten note with his bill:

Dear Sir,
Inasmuch as there are a number of people at your table, I felt that what I had to tell you would be better written than said. I do not make a practice of prying into other people's affairs nor do I whisper in their ear when something of a delicate nature is wrong as I feel this is in very bad taste. Therefore, I have written this note to order to inform you that your fly is open.

Yours truly,
Sam the Waiter

P.S. I love you.

# The Central District

Who is Seattle's favorite rapper?
　　Ice Latte'.

*

What do you call a cubscout troop from the Central District?
　　Boys N The Wood.

*

What's their favorite campfire song?
　　Kum By Yo.

What's the difference between the Central District and Ballard?

    In Ballard, mother is a whole word.

\*

Did you hear FAO Schwarz opened a store in the Central District?

    It's called, "Toys N The Hood."

\*

What does a kid from the Central District get for Christmas?

    My bike.

\*

How can you tell a Mormon in the Central District?

    He's walking.

\*

A young crack dealer was arrested for selling drugs to an undercover narcotics officer. When he was taken before the judge, he pleaded not guilty.

"Not guilty," said the judge. "What is your defense?"

"It was a case of mistaken identity," replied the defendant.

"What do you mean?" asked the judge.

"I didn't know he was a cop."

Who's the Central District's favorite local comedian?
Kunte Keister.

\*

What's "cursive writing" in the Central District?
Spray painting swear words on the wall of a deserted building.

\*

The teacher at a Central District preschool was talking to her class about farming.

"What does the cow say?" she asked.

The first little kid shouted, "Mooooo!"

"That's correct," she replied. "What does the chicken say?"

Another kid shouted, "Cluck, cluck!"

"That's right," said the teacher. "And what does the pig say?"

The third kid said, "FREEZE, SUCKER!"

*"Now explain that to me again, dear.
These homeless people -- why couldn't
they just stay at a hotel?"*

# Bellevue

How do Bellevue yuppies change a lightbulb?
  They put the bulb in the socket and wait for
  the world to revolve around them.

*

Why don't Bellevue housewives have large families?
  Mercedes doesn't make a mini-van.

*

How do Bellevue moms wean their young?
  Fire the babysitter.

What do they call a guy from Bellevue who isn't a lawyer, doesn't drive a Mercedes, and spends a lot of time with his kids?
> A loser.

\*

If noodles are called pasta, what do you call poodles?
> Yappy little bastards.

\*

What is the most popular sorority at Bellevue Community College?
> Gamma Pi Epilady.

\*

A beggar stops a lady in Bellevue and asks for a handout.
> "Please, lady," he says, "I haven't eaten in days."
> The woman says, "You should force yourself."

\*

How can you tell a catholic guy from Bellevue?
> He brings his lawyer to confession.

\*

Why do Bellevue housewives close their eyes during sex?
> So they can pretend they're at the Mall.

What's "bilingual" in Bellevue?
Talking about shopping.

*

What is the Bellevue Kiwanas' new proposal to end World Hunger?
Appetite suppressants.

**■■■■■■ NORTHWEST JEOPARDY ■■■■■■**

**Q:** The first thing a Bellevue housewife does during spring cleaning.

**A:** What is METER MAID?

What's a Bellevue housewife's idea of "roughing it?"
A hotel with no room service.

*

A couple from Bellevue were making love one night when the husband said, "Dear, did I hurt you?"
"No," said the wife. "Why do you ask?"
"Well," said the husband, "For a minute there, I thought you moved."

On their honeymoon night, a young Bellevue husband asked his bride, "Will you love me forever?"

"I will always love you," she answered.

"What if I grow fat and old?"

"I will always love you." she said tenderly.

"What if I get sick and frail?"

"I will always love you," she repeated.

"What if I go broke and lose all my money?"

"I will always love you," said the young bride. "Not only will I love you, but I will miss you."

*

Did you hear about the new Bellevue gang?

    Boys N The Burbs.

*

What's Bellevue's idea of open minded?

    Dating a Canadian.

*

What's the slogan for Bellevue's DARE Program?

    "Just say, 'No, thank you.'"

*

What's the difference between a BMW and a pair of Levi's?

    You can only fit one asshole into a pair of Levi's.

Two Bellevue housewives, Heather and Buffy, were volunteering at the Bellevue Public Library when a nun walked in and asked if they had any cookbooks.

"I'll have to check," said Heather and went into the backroom.

"What's a nun doing in the library?" asked Buffy.

"She said she's looking for a cookbook," said Heather.

"What's a cookbook?" asked Buffy.

"How should I know," replied Heather, "I'm not Catholic."

*"Well, it is waterfront."*

# Tacoma

There once was a guy in a coma
Who woke to a real bad aroma.
He said with a start,
"Did somebody fart?
Or did I just wake up in Tacoma?"

What's the difference between the new Toyota Tacoma
and other small pickup trucks?
No emission control.

Did you hear about President Clinton's visit to
Tacoma?
He didn't inhale.

## ANOTHER ROADSIDE ATTRACTION

# SANITARY
# LANDFILL

### CAUTION
### Oxymorons Ahead

\*

If the Seattle PI were published in Tacoma what would it be called?

The Seattle PU.

\*

What do you fish for in Commencement Bay?

Smelt.

\*

Why did they put the Point Defiance Zoo in Tacoma?

So the skunks would feel at home.

\*

Who's Tacoma's favorite singer?

Fart Garfunkle.

A guy from Tacoma, a guy from Everett and a guy from Seattle were walking past a foul smelling pigsty at the Puyallup Fair. They decided to make a bet on who could stay inside the longest.

After five minutes, the guy from Seattle came out.

After ten minutes, the guy from Everett came out.

After twenty minutes, the pigs came out.

Why is it impossible to walk across Tacoma?

No one can hold their breath that long.

**Don Juan DeLowry**

# Politics

What did Governor Lowry give his staff for the holidays?

A Christmas goose.

How many politicians does it take to screw in a lightbulb?

"I didn't screw anybody."

If Sleeping Beauty lived in Olympia, what would Prince Charming be?

Under investigation.

Governor Lowry showed up at work one morning with a tremendous black eye.

"Governor," asked one of his aides. "What happened?"

"It was just a crazy misunderstanding," replied the governor, shaking his head. "I was standing on the bus minding my own business when I noticed this lady in front of me. She was standing there and her dress was tucked into the crack of her rear end. I decided to help her out so I reached out and gave her dress a little tug and untucked it."

"And that's when she hit you?"

"No that's not when she hit me," replied the Governor. "She turned around and started cussing a blue streak."

"So when did she hit you?" asked the aide.

"Well," said the Governor. "She seemed so upset that I untucked her dress, I reached out and tucked it back in."

✻

**Olympia Bumpersticker**

# Have You Hugged Your Governor Today?

What do you get when you cross the governor with the phone company?

A politician who wants to reach out and touch someone.

*

What do Governor Lowry and Bob Vila have in common?

They're both pretty handy.

*

Why were Governor Lowry's lawyers so concerned about the allegations of sexual misconduct?

He didn't know "harass" was one word.

*

What's the worst thing about local political jokes?

Too many of them get elected.

*

What do an honest politician and Bigfoot have in common?

Nobody has ever seen one.

*

Did you hear about the new watchdog organization looking out for the interests of Washington's fatcats?

It's called, "WashPig."

Slade Gorton was asked during a press conference what made for a successful politician.

"The key to becoming an effective politician," the senator replied, "is to always be sincere -- whether you mean it or not."

*

A tired PI reporter came back to the office after one of Slade Gorton's press conferences.

"Boy, that was a long speech," said the editor.

"Sure was," said the reporter.

"What was it about?" asked the editor.

"I don't know," replied the reporter. "He didn't say."

*

When former House Speaker, Tom Foley, was campaigning for reelection, he came across a little farm in Sprague.

A young boy was milking a cow in the front yard and as they were talking, the boy's mother came to the door and said, "Son, come in the house for dinner!"

And then noticing Foley, she asked, "Who is the fella with you?"

"He says he's a politician," said the boy.

"Well, in that case," she replied, "you'd better bring the cow with you."

## ANOTHER ROADSIDE ATTRACTION

## CAUTION
### Legislative Special Session in Progress

\*

What's the difference between a Special Session and Special Education?
> Some people actually benefit from Special Education.

\*

What's the difference between the State Legislature and the Ringling Brothers Circus?
> At Ringling Brothers, no one takes the clowns seriously.

\*

How can you tell it's winter in Olympia?
> The politicians have their hands in their own pockets.

Two Washington Congressmen are having lunch. The first one says, "I had the weirdest thing happen to me last night. I was confronted by The Devil. Right in my office! He said in exchange for my soul, I could become the next Speaker Of The House."

"Great," says the second one. "What's the catch?"

\*

Did you hear that Seattle's Mayor is sponsoring a new marathon?

It's called Rice-A-Runny.

\*

What do you call the Mayor in a synagogue?
Converted Rice.

\*

What do you call the Mayor in the woods?
Wild Rice.

\*

What do you call Senator Murray on a cattle ranch?
Cow Patty.

\*

What do you get when you cross a Seattle Seahawk with a Washington State Senator?

A politician who can't pass a bill.

What's the difference between the State Legislature and a 4-H Exhibit at the Puyallup Fair?

> The 4-H exhibit is only full of crap for three months of the year.

# Sports

What has eight legs and an I.Q. of 50?

    Four guys watching a Seahawks game?

What has enormous boobs and stands on the sidelines?

    The Seahawks coaching staff.

How many Seahawks does it take to screw in a lightbulb?

    Two. One to screw it in and the other one to recover the fumble.

What sits around the house and goes choo-choo-choo, choo-choo-choo, choo-choo-choo?

Tom Flores on game day.

*

Dennis Erickson was on the sidelines watching scrimmage at the Seahawks spring training camp.

On the first play, a young rookie halfback ran up the middle and was tackled for a loss.

Disgusted with this dismal performance, Erickson hollared, "That's not how you do it! Didn't they teach you anything about running in college? Here, give me the ball! I'll show you how it's done."

The coach stormed out onto the field and lined up with the players.

"Now watch closely. It's not that hard," he said. And with that, the center snapped the ball. The quarterback handed it off and Coach Erickson slammed into the line, smashing right into a pile of enormous defensive players.

When the play was over he looked up and said, "Now do you see how it's supposed to be done?"

"Yes, coach." said the rookie.

"Good!" said the coach. "Now you do it that way from now on! Oh, and one more thing."

"Yes, coach?" answered the rookie.

"Somebody call an ambulance. I think I broke my leg."

## ANOTHER ROADSIDE ATTRACTION

**Warning: Seahawks Ahead.**

*

What's the toughest position to fill on the Seahawks team?
  Designated driver.

*

Did you hear the new Seahawks fight song?
  "99 Bottles of Beer On The Wall."

*

Why is the Seahawk backfield like a Coho Salmon?
  Neither one of them had a good run last year.

*

Why are the Seahawk receivers so healthy?
  They never catch anything.

What keeps the Seahawks from going to the Superbowl?

The other teams..

∗

What do Seagals and cow chips have in common?

The older they get, the easier they are to pick up.

∗

What do you call a fat guy with a temperature of 104?

Husky Fever.

∗

What's the difference between the Huskies and the Seahawks?

The Seahawks get paid by check.

∗

What do you call a Husky with a real job?

Alumni.

∗

What's the most popular frathouse at the WAZZU?

Phi Beta Keggar.

∗

What's WAZZU's shortest graduate program?

Ten days and a couple two day follow-ups.

Why does the Cougar Marching Band always play at halftime?

To keep the cheerleaders from grazing.

*

Why did the Cougar cheerleader have rectangular boobs?

She forgot to take the tissue out of the box.

*

At the Cougar Pep Rally before the Apple Cup, the Coach stepped to the microphone, "Tomorrow, we are going to win! Now give me a W!"

"W!" shouted the players.

"Give me an I!"

"I!" shouted the players.

"Give me an N!"

"N!" shouted the players.

"What's that spell?"

Complete silence.

*

What's tall, white and smells like fish?

Detlef Shrimp.

*

Did you hear about the Sonic's playoff necklace?

It's a choke chain.

What new play has George Carl come up with for this year's playoffs?

The Heimlich Maneuver.

*

What did the Mariners players get from last year's baseball strike?

Fewer losing games.

*

Why are the Mariner's like a Robert Fulghum newspaper column?

They're both usually pointless.

*"Well, frankly no, Lou,
I don't think it's a good idea."*

What's the difference between Ken Griffey Jr. and a frog?

A frog usually catches flies without breaking his arm.

What was the toughest part about Ken Griffey's wrist injury?

Counting all his money with one hand.

When Dave showed up for work on Tuesday, his boss stopped him at the door, "Hey, what's the big idea calling in sick yesterday?"

"I *was* sick," said Dave.

"Oh really?" said the boss. "Well, you didn't look that sick when I saw you at the Mariners game."

"Oh yeah," said Dave. "Well, you should have seen me after that fourth King Beer."

# Seattle
## Then and Now

1965

1995

# Celebrities

Why did Seattle Harbor Tours throw Jean Enersen overboard?

> They heard she was a good anchor.

What do you call a weatherman who makes less than a buck an hour?

> A 99 cent Woppler.

What do "Almost Live!" and a Woodland Park Zoo baboon have in common?

> Every Saturday people come and laugh at their bald keister.

What do you call a KOMO Weatherman in a flood?
A wading poole.

*

What do you call the KOMO Weatherman at work?
An office Poole.

*

What do you call a KOMO Weatherman driving to work?
A car Poole.

*

What's a Northwest surfer's favorite newscaster?
Lori Masukawabunga.

*

When former "Evening Magazine" co-host, Penny LeGate, called the show's producer to begin negotiations on her new contract, she asked, "Where would you like to meet -- my office or yours?"

"Hey," said the producer, "if it's gonna be a hassle, just forget it."

*

What is the difference between an "Evening Magazine" Producer and a terrorist?
You can negotiate with a terrorist.

What's the difference between Steve Raible and Jean Enersen?
  Steve doesn't bleach his moustache.

*

How do you check Shawna McLaughlin's I.Q.?
  Stick a tire gauge in her ear.

*

What does she say when you blow in her ear?
  "Thanks for the refill."

*

Comedian, Ross Shafer, was doing a benefit for Channel 9. When he saw the running order of the show, he noticed that he was following a circus act.
  "Hey," he said to the stage manager. "I'm Ross Shafer! I used to be the host of "Almost Live!" I've toured all over the country! You can't have a star of my caliber on after a bunch of performing monkeys!"
  "Yes, you're right," said the stage manager. "Your acts are rather similar."

*

What's the difference between Cindi Reinhardt and an Amway Salesman?
  After a while, even an Amway salesman will stop yakking about his soaps?

That sports guy named Tony Ventrella
Has an unusual nose for a fella
It works great for snoring
And when it starts pouring
It doubles as an umbrella

✳

An elderly couple was watching Town Meeting one night.

"You know," said the wife, "I read in Pacific Magazine that when Ken Schram started out, he didn't really want to become a serious journalist."

"Well," replied the husband, "it looks like he got his wish."

What do you call it when you throw Town Meeting's host into Elliott Bay?

A Schram Dunk.

\*

What do you get when you cross Town Meeting with Ivars Seafood?

Acres of Schrams.

\*

What do you get when you cross Town Meeting with a pig?

Ken Spam.

\*

Did you hear about Sunny Kobe Cook's new store in Yakima?

It's called "Sheep Country USA."

\*

What would you get if you crossed Jack Roberts with Sunny Kobe Cook?

Some incredibly annoying children.

\*

How can you tell if your house is haunted by the ghost of Curt Cobain?

It smells like teen spirit.

85

What do you get when you cross KUOW with KMPS?
Sandy Bradley's Potgut.

\*

What do you get when you cross KVI Radio with Kentucky Fried Chicken?
A bucket filled with nothing but right-wings and assholes.

\*

What is the difference between Anne Wilson and Nancy Wilson?
About 50 pounds.

\*

Why is Anne Wilson like a can of Campbell's Soup?
They're both "Hot and Chunky."

\*

Why do they classify most of Kenny G's music as "easy listening?"
Because there's not enough room to dance in an elevator.

\*

What's the definition of "endless love?"
Dianne Schuur and Ray Charles out playing tennis.

What's the difference between The Far Side and the first Rapid Transit Proposal?

People bought The Far Side.

\*

Gary Larson, the author of "The Far Side" cartoon strip, was driving through Enumclaw when his car broke down. When he stopped at a gas station to ask for help, he realized that he didn't have his wallet.

When it came time to pay, Gary told the mechanic who he was and what he did for a living, and promised to send him a check. The mechanic thought for a moment and then replied, "The Far Side, huh? I'm afraid we didn't get that around here."

"It was published in over 800 newspapers," said Gary. " I'm surprised you people have never seen it."

"Oh, we *seen* it," said the farmer, rubbing his chin. "We just didn't *get* it."

**Tonight at Eight**

## *FIELD OF SCHEMES*

**King County Executive, Gary Locke, stars as a local politician plagued with voices urging him to spend millions on a new baseball stadium in hopes of improving the Mariners' record. (2 hours)**

# TV Guide

**6pm**   **MOVIE - Drama**
\*\*\* "Don Juan de Fuca" (1995)
The rantings of a young mental patient in-
spire Northwest Salmon to begin spawning
again.

**THE PRICE IS RICE**
Game show contestants try to guess the cost
of the Mayor's new budget.

**7pm**   **MOVIE - Suspense**
\*\*\*\* "Pulp Mill Fiction" (1994)
Quentin Tarentino's dark comedy about a
small woodland creature who single handedly
kills off our state's timber industry.

**8pm** **GAYWATCH**
David Hasselhoff stars as a lifeguard assigned to Volunteer Park.

**VANISHING SUN**
A young martial arts master wanders around the Northwest looking for blue skies.

**9pm** **MOVIE - Action Adventure**
**1/2 "The River Mild" (1994)
Meryl Streep, Kevin Bacon. Terrifying tale of a family's attempt to go whitewater rafting through the Ballard Locks.

**UNSOLVED MISERIES**
Tragic stories of local suffering: child abuse, murder, suicide, and a man who was trapped in an elevator with Jack Roberts.

**MOVIE - Comedy Drama**
*** "A Log of Their Own" (1993)
Tom Hanks, Geena Davis. Light-hearted look at an all-girl timber camp during WWII.

**10pm** **MOVIE - Drama**
*** "Raible Without a Cause." (1968)
James Dean stars as a troubled youth who wishes to become a local TV newsanchor.

**11pm  TOWN MATING**
Orgy at Ken Schram's house.

**MOVIE - Adventure**
\*\*\*\* "The Hunt For Red Tide Oysters"
Russian submarine gets lost in Hood Canal.

**MURRAY SHE WROTE**
Angela Lansbury as a Northwest Senator.

---

**Close Up**

**Sunday 8pm**     **Lewis and Cluck**

Jean Auel's sweeping novel finally comes to the screen in this bold 12 part PBS Series that chronicles the travels of Lewis and Cluck, a man and his chicken, who explored around the Pacific Northwest during the mid-1800's. Peter Strauss, Richard Chamberlin. (2 hours)

**It was apparent from the outset that Bill
would not work out at Boeing.**

# Boeing

What do Boeing and Volume Shoe Source have in common?

    100,000 loafers.

What do you call a Boeing employee who sleeps through his lunch hour?

    An overachiever.

If Rip Van Winkle woke up at Boeing, what would he get?

    Back pay.

A young Boeing engineer looked up from his desk and asked his boss, "I know this is going to sound stupid, but how many degrees are in a circle?"

"Well, that depends," said the boss, "How big is the circle?"

\*

Another engineer was working over a set of blueprints.

"Hey, boss," he said, looking up from the drawings, "how many thousandths in an inch?"

"Gee," replied the boss. "There must be millions of them."

\*

Two Boeing engineers were moving their office to a new floor. After several hours of struggling with a big desk on the stairs, the first one said, "It's no use. We'll never get it up these stairs."

"Up?" replied the second engineer. "I thought we were going down."

\*

After finding several members of his crew in a backroom playing cards, the foreman asked, "Isn't there something else you could be doing?"

"Well," shrugged one of the workers. "I guess there's checkers."

## ANOTHER ROADSIDE ATTRACTION

## BOEING EMPLOYMENT CENTER

\*

During contract negotiations, the Boeing Union Representative held a press conference.

"Working conditions are intolerable," he said. "The hours are long, the pay is low and collective bargaining is getting us nowhere."

"Why don't you strike?" asked the reporter.

"We tried that once," replied the Union Rep, "but it took almost three weeks before management even noticed."

\*

How many Boeing workers does it take to screw in a lightbulb?

It can't be done.

# The
## Department of Justice
## "New Math" Quiz

## QUESTION
If little Johnny has a third
of the apple and little
Susie has a third
of the apple,
what does
littleBilly
have?

## ANSWER
An unfair advantage.

# Microsoft

Did you hear about the new Microsoft home game?
It's called "Monopoly."

Bill Gates hired a prestigious Seattle law firm to defend Microsoft against a recent antitrust suit. After months of litigation, the head attorney called him at home.

"Mr. Gates," he said, "justice has prevailed!"

"Really?" said Gates. "Then you'd better file an appeal immediately."

What do you call a troll with a billion dollars?
Billy Gates Gruff.

*

What do you call it when Bill Gates wins the lottery?
Redundant.

*

What does Bill Gates call his wife?
MRS-Dos.

*

Where does Bill Gates buy his clothes?
Nerdstroms.

*

What do you get when you cross Bill Gates with a vampire?
The Byte Of Seattle.

*

What do Microsoft employees do in their spare time?
"What's 'spare time?'"

*

Why do Microsoft employees wish Bill Gates would become The Godfather?
Then they'd only have to kiss his ring.

How many Microsoft employees does it take to screw in a lightbulb?

None. That's a hardware problem.

✻

What's the first sign the guy installing Windows on your new computer is not an authorized repairman?

He's using putty.

*"Seems like more of a threat than a promise."*

# Those Little Town Blues

What's the most enjoyable way to view the sights of Renton?

Through your rearview mirror.

*

Did you hear they're opening a Uwajimawa's in Everett?

Home Cooked Sushi.

*

Why do so many guys from Issaquah drive 4x4's?

It reminds them of the last math equation they ever solved.

What's the hardest part about living in Bothell?
> Trying to sound macho when you tell people where you're from.

*

In Chehalis, what's the difference between a bank and a family tree?
> A bank usually has several branches.

*

Did you hear about Bellingham International Airport's new security system?
> A guy with a horseshoe magnet and a pair of X-Ray specs.

*

What's the last thing a Renton stripper takes off?
> Her bowling shoes.

*

How do Ellensburg insomniacs count sheep?
> "She loves me, she loves me not, she loves me, she loves me not ..."

*

What's the easiest way to get to Walla Walla?
> First you commit a felony. Then you get a court appointed lawyer.

Said a young Californian named Murph
After going to Westport to surf.
"The waves are a hoot
But without a wetsuit
You come out looking just like a Smurf."

*

What do you call two Westport surfers in January?
Numb and Number.

*

Why was the North Bend math teacher arrested for indecent exposure?
He was trying to count to eleven.

*

How many people does it take to make chocolate chip cookies in Yakima?
Two. One stirs the batter. The other one squeezes the rabbit.

*

What does I.Q. stand for in Omak?
Intelligence Thingamabob.

*

What have they banned Rap Music in Buckley?
People kept trying to squaredance.

**103**

What's the best time to see the harvest moon in Ritzville?

> When a wheat farmer bends over to work on his tractor.

\*

Why do they call the town "Ritzville?"

> Because it's full of crackers.

\*

What's the most popular home improvement project in Goldendale?

> Rotating your tires.

\*

Why do people from Maple Valley scratch their butts?

> To stimulate their minds.

\*

Three guys are standing in line at Taco Bell. How can you tell which one is from Black Diamond?

> He's the one trying to buy a phone.

\*

Why have they stopped christening babies in the Port Angeles Catholic Church?

> The kids rarely survive getting hit in the head with a champagne bottle.

**Curbside Recycling in the Tri-Cities**

What's the Number One song in Hanford?
Glowin' In The Wind.

*

What is the favorite food in the Tri-Cities?
The Patty Meltdown.

*

What's the difference between Hanford and Boeing?
At the Hanford company picnic, the three-legged race is considered a solo event.

**105**

What's the first sign that a Hanford worker has been exposed to too much radiation?

>She gets testicle cancer.

\*

Why is it so easy to get a job after working at Hanford?

>You always get a glowing recommendation.

\*

How can you tell a wine connoisseur from Elma?

>He's the one sniffing the screw top.

\*

How can you tell a wine connoisseur from Humptulips?

>He's the one drinking beer.

\*

Why do girls from Aberdeen wear turtlenecks?

>To hide their flea collars.

\*

How do Sequim investors diversify their portfolios?

>Putting their money in both Quinto and Lotto.

\*

Did you hear about the guy from Eatonville who thought homogenized milk came from gay cattle?

What do Whatcom County neo-nazi's drive to their rallies?
>The Chrysler KKK Car.

\*

What's the definition of "politically correct" in Whatcom County?
>Equal opportunity for all White Anglo Saxon Protestants regardless of their race, creed or color.

\*

What is the definition of the word "ambidextrous" in Wenatchee?
>Picking your nose with both hands.

\*

Why did they close down the Arlington Library?
>Somebody lost the book.

\*

Did you hear about the new Renton Stairmaster class?
>Running up the down escalator at J.C. Pennys.

\*

What do you call a guy from Sprague with a sheep under one arm and a pig under the other?
>Bisexual.

**Recent Lotto winner, Delbert Stumpf,
considers his future.**

What do you call a guy from Vantage with indoor plumbing?

Pretentious.

\*

How does a Puyallup girl break up with her boyfriend?

She sends him a John Deere letter.

What's green, red, purple, orange, brown, pink and covered with polka dots?
>A lady from Sumner dressed up for church.

\*

Why did the guy from Montesano pick his nose with a spoon?
>He heard that it was impolite to eat with your fingers.

\*

>There once was a guy from Spokane
>Who apparently ate too much bran
>He said, "Just me luck!
>Now I'm gonna be stuck
>For the rest of my life in the can."

\*

What do they mean by the "Longview Limbo?"
>Seeing how low your pants can hang in back.

\*

What's a good solution to the crack problem in Elma?
>Suspenders.

\*

What's long and hard on a guy from Centralia?
>The third grade.

What do the Mayor of Moses Lake and Mr. Peanut have in common?
> They're both goobers.

*

What are the four basic food groups in Mount Vernon?
> Two-thirds of a six-pack.

*

What's Lynden's idea of higher education?
> A grade school with a second floor.

*

What's the hardest part about going to grade school in Milton?
> Finding a babysitter for your kids.

*

What's the most popular marriage proposal in Kent?
> "You're gonna have a *what?*"

*

What does 501 stand for?
> The collective I.Q. of Vancouver.

*

What's the difference between Kelso and Mars?
> There could be intelligent life on Mars.

Did you hear about the guy from Duvall who was killed during a pie eating contest?
A cow stepped on his head.

What's the nicest thing about living in Spokane?
At least it's not Idaho.

"B-13."

# The Great Outdoors

What do you get when you cross a Spotted Owl with a Chinook Salmon?

    100% unemployment in Grays County.

What do you call it when a Spotted Owl poops in the forest?

    Endangered feces.

If Paul Bunyon lived in Grays Harbor County, what would he be?

    Out of work.

What's the newest creature to be added to the endangered species list?

Northwest loggers.

**xxxxx NORTHWEST JEOPARDY xxxxx**

**Q:** What makes Weyerhauser employees such good dancers.

**A:** What is "LOGARITHM?"

A tourist who saw Mount Rainer
Was shocked the people 'round here
Would spend all of their time
Building this sign
Just to advertise beer

\*

Two old guys are fishing off the dock. For hours neither one moves a muscle.

Then finally, after his foot falls asleep, one of them wiggles his toes slightly.

"Dammit," says the other one, "did you come here to fish or to dance?"

*"Knock it off, Larry, can't you see you're
just encouraging them."*

What do you get when you cross Eddie Bauer with
Levi Strauss?

    A guy who wants to hike up his pants.

\*

What's brown and runny and smells like Gortex?

    DiahREI.

\*

What's a slug's favorite TV show?

    "Almost Slime!"

**115**

An old man was hiking along the Pacific Crest Trail when he came across a little frog in a pond. He picked it up and was surprised to hear the frog say, "I'm a talking frog."

"That's amazing," said the old guy, "a talking frog!"

"Not only that," said the frog, "if you kiss me, I will turn into a beautiful blonde woman."

"That's amazing," repeated the old man. Then he put the little frog in his pocket and walked along.

After awhile the frog stuck his head out and said, "Didn't you hear me? I said if you kiss me I will turn into a beautiful blonde."

"Oh I heard you," said the old guy. "It's just that, at my age, sometimes you prefer a talking frog."

\*

What's big and slimey, has ten legs and runs through the forest?

A Sasquid.

\*

What's the most dangerous invertebrate in the woods?

A .45 Caliber Slug.

\*

What does Bigfoot wear to tell time?

A saswatch.

## ANOTHER ROADSIDE ATTRACTION

Deer
Crossing

Deer Auditioning for
the Pacific NW Ballet

Deer
On Steroids

Two old fisherman are sitting around talking.

One says, "Hey, I just got a new fishing pole for my wife."

The other one says, "Good trade."

---

**NORTHWEST JEOPARDY**

**Q:** What Grace Kelly did to become a princess.

**A:** What is "MOUNT RAINIER?"

---

118

What's green and swims up the Ballard Locks?
    Herschel, The Sea Lime.

*

What do you get when you cross a skinhead with an environmentalist?
    A guy who wants to shave the whales.

**RENTONITE: A mineral from the Kryptonite family that doesn't kill Superman, but does cause him to suffer from acute boredom.**

# Northwest Names

## ASOTIN
The silver coating found on losing
Scratch Lottery Tickets.

## BANGOR
An abnormally large mole usually
with a hair growing out of it.

## BELLINGHAM
The gelatinous substance that surrounds
a canned meat product.

## BUMBERSHOOT
The momentary embarrassment a deer hunter feels when that four-point buck he was aiming at turns out to be a Heifer.

## CARKEEK
A person who drives for more than a block with his turn indicator on. (Usually found, either in Ballard, or driving to and from Ballard.)

## CATHLAMET
The metal crossbar that is on boy's bicycle for no reason other than to cause a great deal of pain when they slip off the seat and land on it.

## CHEWELAH
Any food particle lodged in your front teeth.

## COWLITZ
The rubber nozzles on a milking machine.

## DOSEWALLIPS
The little baseball bat used by fishermen to render fish unconscious after pulling them into the boat.

## DUWAMISH
Adjective referring to the backup "do-wah" vocals found in most popular songs from the fifties.

## DUWAMPS
The little reflective bumps on the center line of most highways.

## GRAND COULEE
The leader of the Asian Ku Klux Klan.

## HOQUIUM
Seattle native who wears sunglasses all year long.

## ILWACO
A mentally ill Spaniard.

## KENNEWICK
That little string that hangs from a Tampon.

## KLICKITAT
Technical term for a TV Remote Control..

## LESCHI
A dialect spoken by winos soliciting funds in Pioneer Square.

## LAURELHURST
Any Seafair float sponsored by a funeral home.

## MADRONA
Any conversation with Cindi Reinhardt.

## MOCLIPS
An electric razor used for trimming nose hairs.

## NAPAVINE
That maze of ropes at Seafirst Bank that give you the impression that you're standing in line for a ride at Disneyland.

## NESPELEM
The sound made by a latte machine.

## NOOKSACK
A small leather garment worn by Indian Braves during athletic events.

## PAULSBO
The knot bakers tie in Bavarian pretzels.

## PUYALLUP
What's left of an animal after it's been run over by a Mack truck.

## PYSHT
The feeling a panhandler gets when you ignore him.

## QUEETS
That little squeaking noise your sinuses make after you've blown your nose really hard.

## RAVENNA

The vertical crease on a woman's abdomen from wearing pantyhose.

## REARDAN

Any person who wears adult diapers underneath a pair of tight jeans.

## SEDRO WOOLLEY

The synthetic fabric used in the manufacture of imitation lambskin seatcovers.

## SEMIAHMOO

Chinese word meaning "small cow."

## SEQUIM

What squids do in the water.

## SHILSHOLE

A person who considers the Lotto to be a valid investment plan.

## SKYKOMISH

The peculiar odor that emanates from pulp mills.

## SKAGIT

Any food left in the refrigerator long enough to begin supporting new life forms.

### SNOHOMISH
Cabin fever experienced by parents when school is officially closed due to inclement weather.

### SPANAWAY
Any missing chunk of guardrail along the road.

### SQUALICUM
The sound made by someone running their fingernails down a chalkboard.

### STILLAGUAMISH
Any foreign substance found on the underside of a table or countertop.

### SUMAS
The part of a trucker's butt that sticks out of his jeans when he is changing a tire.

### SUQUAMISH
What's left of a slug after you pour salt on it.

### TATOOSH
Anyone who has their present boyfriend's name tattooed on their butt.

### TULALIP
A flower grown in Hollaland.

## TUMWATER
The liquid that collects in your bellybutton
while sunbathing.

## TWISP
The remaining hair on John Keister's head.

## TYEE
The rubberband that Wallingford guys use
to hold their ponytails in place.

## WAPATO
The one lopsided wheel found on grocery carts
that causes them to drive erratically.

## WASHOUGAL
Anyone who peeks at others while they are bathing.

## WINLOCK
A psychological condition that prevents the Sonics
from succeeding in the playoffs.